# This Is What I Want to Be

# Cowboy

## Heather Miller

Heinemann Library
Chicago, Illinois

Customer Service  888-454-2279
Visit our website at www.heinemannlibrary.com

Designed by Sue Emerson, Heinemann Library
Printed and bound in the United States by Lake Book Manufacturing, Inc.

07 06 05 04 03
10 9 8 7 6 5 4 3 2 1

**Library of Congress Cataloging-in-Publication Data**
Miller, Heather.
    Cowboy / Heather Miller.
      p. cm. — (This is what I want to be)
Includes index.
Contents: What do cowboys do? — What is a cowboy's day like? — What do cowboys wear? — What tools do cowboys use? — Where do cowboys work? — When do cowboys work? — Do cowboys work in other places? — What special jobs do cowboys do? — How do people become cowboys? — Quiz.
    ISBN: 1-4034-0366-X (HC), 1-4034-0588-3 (Pbk.)
    1.  Cowboys—West (U.S.)—Juvenile literature. 2.  Ranch life—West (U.S.)—Juvenile literature. 3.  West (U.S.)—Social life and customs—Juvenile literature. [1. Cowboys. 2. Occupations.]  I. Title.
    F596.M63 2002
    636.21'3'0978—dc21

                            2001008133

**Acknowledgments**
The author and publishers are grateful to the following for permission to reproduce copyright material:
pp. 4, 17, 20 David Stoecklein Photography; p. 5 Ted Grant/Masterfile; p. 6 Paul Chesley/Stone/Getty Images; p. 7 Paul A. Souders/Corbis; p. 8 Adam Smith/FPG International; p. 9 Randy Wells/Stone/Getty Images; p. 10L David Stoecklein/ Corbis Stock Market; pp. 10R, 23 Hot Ideas/Index Stock Imagery, Inc.; p. 11 Kit Houghton/Corbis; p. 12 Joseph Sohm/ChromoSohm Inc./Corbis; p. 13 Richard T. Rowan/Photo Researchers, Inc.; p. 14 Dave Rosenberg/Index Stock Imagery, Inc.; p. 15 Robert Y. Ono/Corbis Stock Market; p. 16 Kevin Dodge/Masterfile; p. 18 Michael S. Lewis/Corbis; p. 19 Corbis Stock Market; p. 21 Tim Davis/Photo Researchers, Inc.; p. 23 (row 1, L-R) Kit Houghton/Corbis, Ted Grant/ Masterfile, Paul Chesley/Stone/Getty Images, Joseph Sohm/ChromoSohm Inc./Corbis; p. 23 (row 2, L-R) Hot Ideas/Index Stock Imagery, Inc., Randy Wells/Stone/Getty Images, Hot Ideas/Index Stock Imagery, Inc., Robert Y. Ono/Corbis Stock Market; p. 23 (row 3, L-R) Walt Anderson/Visuals Unlimited, Richard T. Rowan/Photo Researchers, Inc., David Stoecklein/ Corbis Stock Market, Robert Y. Ono/Corbis Stock Market; p. 23 (row 4) Michael S. Lewis/Corbis

Cover photograph by Ted Grant/Masterfile
Photo research by Scott Braut

Special thanks to our advisory panel for their help in the preparation of this book:

Eileen Day, Preschool Teacher
Chicago, IL

Ellen Dolmetsch, MLS
Wilmington, DE

Kathleen Gilbert,
Second Grade Teacher
Austin, TX

Sandra Gilbert,
Library Media Specialist
Houston, TX

Angela Leeper,
Educational Consultant
North Carolina Department
of Public Instruction
Raleigh, NC

Pam McDonald, Reading Teacher
Winter Springs, FL

Melinda Murphy,
Library Media Specialist
Houston, TX

We would also like to thank K. T. Nelson for reviewing the contents of this book for accuracy.

Some words are shown in bold, **like this.**
You can find them in the picture glossary on page 23.

# Contents

# What Do Cowboys Do?

Cowboys raise horses and **cattle**.

Cowboys ride horses.

They herd cattle.

# What Is a Cowboy's Day Like?

hay

Cowboys give the animals **hay** to eat.

They give them water to drink.

Cowboys take care of their horses.

This cowboy is changing a **horseshoe.**

# What Do Cowboys Wear?

hat

chaps

Cowboys wear clothes that keep them warm and dry.

Cowboy hats keep out the sun, rain, and snow.

**Chaps** keep their legs safe from sharp **burrs.**

Boots cover their feet.

# What Tools Do Cowboys Use?

Cowboys use a **lasso** to catch **cattle**.

They mark the **calves** with a **branding iron**.

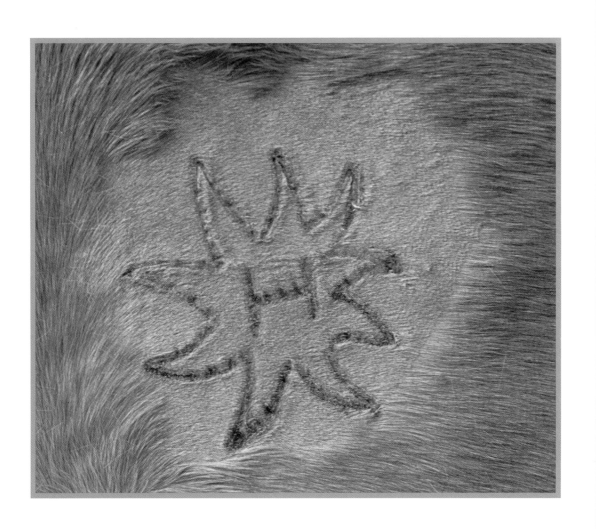

The mark is called a **brand.**

Brands tell cowboys which cattle belong to them.

# Where Do Cowboys Work?

Cowboys work on **ranches**.

A ranch has a lot of land.

After work, cowboys eat in the **cookhouse**.

# Do Cowboys Work in Other Places?

Sometimes cowboys work far out on the **ranch**.

They sleep outside and cook on a campfire.

Some cowboys go to **rodeos**.

This cowboy is roping a **steer**
at a rodeo.

# When Do Cowboys Work?

Cowboys work every day.

They wake up very early in the morning.

They work when it is hot or cold.

They work in rain or snow.

# What Special Jobs Do Cowboys Do?

Cowboys sometimes help when new **calves** are born.

They make sure the mother and calf are healthy.

Cowboys look for lost **cattle**.

This cowboy is looking for a lost calf.

# How Do People Become Cowboys?

Cowboys learn from other cowboys.

Some children learn to be cowboys from their parents.

They learn to ride horses.

When the children grow up,
they will run the **ranch.**

# Quiz

Can you remember what these things are called?

Look for the answers on page 24.

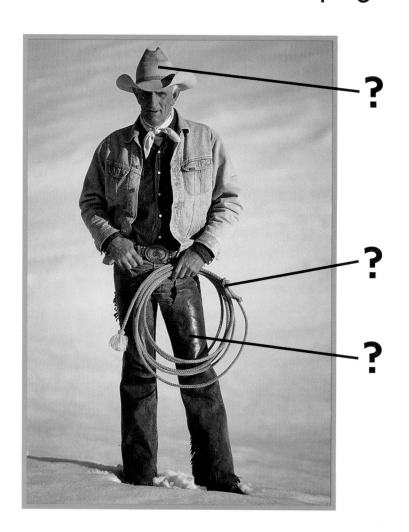

?

?

?

# Picture Glossary

**brand**
page 11

**cattle**
pages 4, 5,
10, 11, 19

**hay**
page 6

**ranch**
pages 12, 14, 21

**branding
iron**
page 10

**chaps**
page 9

**horseshoe**
page 7

**rodeo**
page 15

**burr**
page 9

**cookhouse**
page 13

**lasso**
page 10

**steer**
page 15

**calf** (more than
one are **calves**)
pages 10, 18, 19

# Note to Parents and Teachers

Reading for information is an important part of a child's literacy development. Learning begins with a question about something. Help children think of themselves as investigators and researchers by encouraging their questions about the world around them. Each chapter in this book begins with a question. Read the question together. Look at the pictures. Talk about what you think the answer might be. Then read the text to find out if your predictions were correct. Think of other questions you could ask about the topic, and discuss where you might find the answers. Assist children in using the picture glossary and the index to practice new vocabulary and research skills.

# Index

### Answers to quiz on page 22

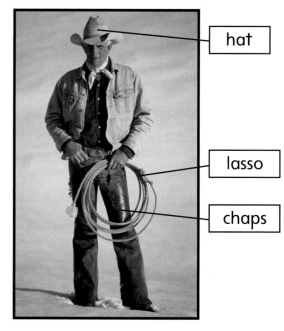

hat

lasso

chaps